The moral rights of the author are asserted. All rights reserved. The moral rights of the author are asserted.

All rights reserved. No part of this book may be reproduced by any mechanical, photographic or electronic process, or in the form of a phonographic recording nor may be stored in a retrieval system, transmitted or otherwise be copied for public or private use, other than for 'fair use' as brief quotations embodied in articles and reviews, without prior written permission of the publisher.

Although every precaution has been taken in preparing this book, the publisher and author assume no responsibility for errors or omissions. Neither is any liability assumed for damages resulting from the use of information contained herein. The moral rights of the author are asserted.

Copyright © 2025 Steve Richardson
All rights reserved.

WITH THANKS TO JULIE

Your presence throughout this journey has been a quiet constant, a steady light when the path was unclear.

Thank you for your wisdom, encouragement, and belief in this work... and in me.

This book would not be what it is without you.

CONTENTS

	Introduction	v
1	A Stranger in a Strange Land	10
2	What is the Soul?	14
3	Beware the enemy of our soul	25
4	What is it the Soul Really wants?	47
5	Let Go – Stop Holding On	56
6	Walking Each Other Home	65
7	Trailing Clouds of Glory	75
8	Listening To Your Soul's Voice	88
9	Not Blinded by The Light	106
10	A Step Forward – A Step Inward	121

FOR

The silent pilgrims of the heart -
those who wander not in search of answers,
but in remembrance of something sacred they
once knew.

To those who feel the ache of exile from their true
home, who long for stillness in a restless world,
and yearn to live with open hearts,
rooted in truth, guided by love.

May these words help you remember who you are:
a soul on a holy journey,
already held, already home.

Veritatis Quaerentibus

INTRODUCTION

The soul is a shimmer of the infinite cloaked in human breath, a whisper from realms unseen, guiding us through the illusion of mortality with echoes of a truth too ancient and sacred to name...

There comes a time in every life when the outer noise grows too loud, and the soul begins to stir. It may come as restlessness, a quiet ache, or a yearning for something deeper - something more meaningful than the routines we perform or the roles we play.

What follows is not a doctrine, but a journey. A gentle encouragement to return to the part of you that has never left - your soul. This book is not here to teach, instruct, or persuade. It is here to remind.

We arrive in this world as infants, unaware of who we are or what path awaits us. As life unfolds, we journey through calm seas and stormy waters, twists and turns, blessings and trials.

Yet what often goes unrecognised is that this journey is not merely physical or emotional - it is deeply spiritual.

PILGRIMAGE OF THE SOUL

We are born with bodies that move, minds that think, and hearts that feel. But beneath it all is the soul: the quiet centre of our being, the wellspring of our deepest truth. It is from the soul that a meaningful life flows.

That small, inner voice - so easily drowned out by the noise of the world, holds the essence of who we are. Though unseen, it is as vital as breath. It does not boast or plead; it whispers.

In stillness, when the ego is quiet and the world recedes, the soul speaks through intuition, compassion, service to others, and the quiet knowing that we are more than we appear to be.

To walk with the soul is to walk in truth. Yet the path is not without challenge. The ego resists stillness and surrender. The world rewards performance over presence. The mind prioritises intellect over intuition. And our busy lives seem always to demand more - even when the soul desires nothing.

But those who learn to listen within find a deeper peace and a more abiding joy not rooted in outward success, but in inner connection.

This peace brings clarity, healing, and love. It reveals the soul's limitless potential when grounded in self-love.

Self-judgement, born of the ego, clouds this truth and disturbs our peace. Every step toward the soul is a step away from fear and a movement closer to love.

In my professional role, I witness how often this inner tension plays out. The emotional duality of fear and love is a constant feature in many lives. When fear becomes dominant, love for self and others begins to fade.

With that absence, we see the emergence of widespread dysfunction, not just individually, but collectively. The need to return to our soul-centre has never been more urgent.

Though our human journey may meander through highs and lows, the soul follows faithfully, with one destination in sight: to return to its eternal home.

And it will return. Shaped and deepened by the human experience, yet unchanged at its core. The soul's essence is pure love - without beginning or end, incapable of increase or decrease. It is constant, unchanging, and forever.

In the end, it is not titles, possessions, or accolades that define us, but the light we carry and the love we share. The quiet legacy of a life lived from within.

This book is for the seeker. For the one who longs to hear the voice within. To rediscover that spark of divinity and to walk a path lit from the inside out.

CHAPTER ONE
A stranger in a strange land

The real voyage of discovery consists not in seeking new landscapes, but in having new eyes."
Marcel Proust

Over the centuries - perhaps millennia - individuals and communities have undertaken pilgrimages.

The word pilgrimage finds its roots in the Latin word, *peregrinus* meaning foreigner or traveller.

Originally, *peregrinus* referred to someone journeying through land not their own - a stranger or wanderer.

From its inception, the word pilgrimage has carried more than the idea of travel. It has always implied a sacred journey; one that transforms the traveller inwardly as much as outwardly.

The pilgrim is not simply visiting a destination, but seeking transformation, truth, or a deepened union with the Divine.

Now, you may not see yourself as a pilgrim. After all, you might not consider yourself on any particular quest. But may I gently suggest that you are?

I base this bold assertion on two truths. First, something - someone, a moment, or a feeling has drawn you to this book. Second, there exists within every human heart a quiet yearning to find meaning and purpose in life.

This purpose - this mission, if you will, is what Emily Dickinson once hinted at when she wrote: *"Narcotics cannot still the Tooth / That nibbles at the soul."*

The soul nibbles at the human heart to remind us that beyond the routines and demands of our work-centric lives, it is on a pilgrimage.

It walks foreign ground, for this earthly life is not its true home. And yet, knowing the challenges of this terrain, the soul chose to come. It longed to grow, to see with new eyes, to love more deeply - for that is its natural disposition.

After all, are you not absorbing everything that crosses your path? Every connection you make in this life reveals more about who you are.

Before we go further, may I invite you to pause for a moment?

Breathe.

Feel the quiet rhythm of life moving through you. Beneath the thoughts, the plans, and the distractions, there is something quieter still.

A presence.

A knowing.

That is your soul.

It walks beside you, not ahead, not behind - just here, gently reminding you of something easily forgotten: that this life is not random, and your path is not without purpose.

You are not simply passing through time. You are returning - step by sacred step, to the deeper truth of who you are.

As you walk through the human experience with all its dense energy, diverse emotions, and multi-faceted relationships - you are, in turn, informing your soul.

PILGRIMAGE OF THE SOUL

As a being of pure light, you cannot experience this terrestrial realm except through a body. And so, the pilgrimage you are on is unique, sacred, and deeply personal.

As a final thought, from one pilgrim to another - may I urge you to treat your fellow travellers with honour, respect, and love. Like you, they are making their pilgrimage along paths you do not know.

And as with all true pilgrimages, we must eventually remember that we return to our eternal home carrying only our experiences, deeds, and learning.

For this is the very reason we left home - to walk this foreign land, and to grow. And always, the soul remembers: you can never be lost, never forgotten, and never truly alone.

CHAPTER TWO
What is the soul?

The one thing in the world of value, is, the active soul, - the soul, free, sovereign, active. This every man is entitled to; this every man contains within him, although, in almost all men, obstructed, and as yet unborn.
~ Ralph Waldo Emerson ~

I've always found it quietly profound that, at funerals, we say, "*May his soul rest in peace.*" The words fall gently, like petals laid on a grave - soft, solemn, final.

They offer comfort to the living, a hope that, at last, the soul has found stillness beyond the noise of this world. But beneath the kindness of the phrase, I find myself wondering: do we speak of peace in death because we sense its absence in life?

Is the soul, in its earthly journey, not already at rest? Or does it strain beneath the weight of fear, expectations, and a search for purpose? Is it caught in the tides of desire, duty, and distraction - always reaching, always wandering?

Perhaps the human soul is like a bird confined - singing through the bars, dreaming of a sky it cannot quite touch.

And so, the question must be asked: What is that ineffable quality we call the soul?

Religion, philosophy, mysticism, and even psychology all offer perspectives on what the soul might be. What they seem to agree upon is that it is not the body – it is something else.

This *'something else'* has been described in many ways - breath, prana, spirit, God's essence, or cosmic energy.

Whatever the name, the soul is often placed above the body and mind; seen as superior, more enduring, more mysterious.

Yet that's no small claim, especially when we consider how remarkably the body serves us, absorbing the countless demands and disturbances we impose upon it, whether through our choices, the actions of others, or the world around us.

Equally, our mind – our thinking power, is no slouch when it comes to helping us navigate our modern world and inventing novel innovations to improve our lot. However, the soul is not the mind or the body.

And whereas we can fully experience the mind and body carrying out their forms and functions - both mentally and physically -this does not hold true for the soul.

Or does it?

The soul, although considered by many to exist, lacks meaningful evidential substance. It cannot be felt like the body, nor does it, at first glance, speak to us in the same way the mind does.

The soul's existence must be accepted through faith; a concept considered an anathema to many due to its religious connotations.

Equally, science encourages us to seek proof of the soul through empirical means. Yet despite carefully monitored studies at the moment of death, no instrument has captured the soul's departure - no photograph, no measurable shift in weight, as though Spirit were something material, something bound by mass.

The closest science has come to proving the existence of the soul is the quantum brain hypothesis, but such a theory does not constitute substantive concrete evidence.

In the search for the soul, one might turn to esoteric practices, drawn by the abundant evidence gathered from reports, research, and individual testimonies related to reincarnation, past life regression through hypnotherapy, mediumship, and near-death experiences.

Of course, esoterica, by its very nature, will at the very least raise a doubtful eyebrow in the sceptic and, at worst, provoke vitriolic trolling. It seems our modern minds rely heavily on proof before anything can truly be believed.

Yet, paradoxically, we often accept certain truths at face value without demanding rigorous evidence.

We believe in the continuity of gravity keeping us grounded, in the persistence of time moving forward, and in the reliability of memory despite its occasional flaws.

We also trust in abstract concepts like justice, loyalty, and identity—fundamental parts of human experience that cannot be quantified or empirically measured.

We accept these certainties instinctively, guided more by experience and collective understanding than by scientific proof.

So, to truly understand the soul, we must look beyond religion, philosophy, science, and even the esoteric. The only reliable authority on this matter is not found in external sources, but within ourselves.

We are the ultimate witnesses and interpreters of our own soul.

To fully understand what the soul is, we must recognise that there is, and must be, a connection to both the mind and the body. To illustrate this point, I'd like to use a nautical metaphor.

The soul is the billowing sail, unfurled to catch the divine breath that moves through all things - a quiet wind of purpose, grace, and higher knowing, an unseen force that moves us without full understanding.

The mind is the tiller, interpreting those subtle shifts and steering us according to reason, thought, and intent.

PILGRIMAGE OF THE SOUL

The body is the vessel, strong yet impermanent, carrying us across the vast ocean of earthly life.

Just as a yacht relies on the harmony between sail, tiller, and hull to navigate the open sea, so too must our soul, mind, and body work in concert to chart a meaningful course through life.

When the soul, mind, and body move in harmony, we are no longer adrift, we become aligned with the deeper current of our spirit, guided not merely by will but by something eternally beautiful within us.

It is only when we truly listen to the soul that we glimpse intimations of who and what we truly are. We begin to understand that there are no boundaries, no limitations, no words or feelings vast enough to contain the majesty and potential within.

But where does this infinite potential originate? What is its true genesis?

While science tells us that we are composed of stardust - our atoms forged in the hearts of ancient stars - this mineral-based perspective only hints at the profound truth of our existence.

Beyond the physical, we are expressions of a greater consciousness, intricately woven into the fabric of the universe.

As manifestations of Source energy - whether called God, YHWH, Allah, the Great Spirit, or I AM - we embody a perfection that transcends mere material origins.

Our essence is not limited to the cosmic particles that form our bodies but is deeply rooted in the divine spark that animates our souls.

However, the soul on its own cannot fulfil its purpose in mortality unless the mind, the active agent of the soul, is in harmonious connection with it.

When the mind is not in concert with the soul, we may say it is *of two minds*. We can go further and suggest that the mind can be either right or wrong, depending on the voice to which it listens.

Right-mindedness listens to the quiet whisperings of the soul, while wrong-mindedness is attuned to the loud bellowing of the ego. An ego content to create illusions, habits and defence mechanisms steeped in judgment, fear, resentment, shame, and loss – to name but a few.

In this world, the only remaining freedom is the freedom of choice; always between two paths, two voices.

Simply put, we may choose to listen to and act upon the soul's guiding voice, or we can serve the capricious nature of the ego.

It is our consciousness that serves as the receptive mechanism, receiving messages from above or below, from the inner spirit or the ego.

One offers true happiness, meaning, and purpose; the other leaves us with an underlying sense that our life deserves so much more. One is rooted in love and acceptance; the other breeds fear and disconnection from oneself and others.

The soul is our universal connection to the Source and, by direct extension, to one another. It is pure loving intent, desiring only the highest good for ourselves and others. A truth reflected in sublime and everyday acts of kindness, sacrifice, love, courage, truth and service.

Unfortunately, when we act against this intent, we invite disharmony and discontent into our lives and often into the lives of others as well.

Thus, the maxim that what we do to another, we also do to ourselves has held true since the dawn of humanity.

The soul is harmonious, loving and peaceful. In the same way the Source brings order and balance to the cosmos and all it contains, so too do our souls seek to bring order and peace to our lives.

And when we recognise that the soul is eternal, the illusions generated by the ego about our mortal identity are revealed as a mirage: unreal, fleeting, and ultimately, meaningless. Something C.S. Lewis understood when he said, "*You don't have a soul. You are a soul. You have a body.*"

When we live from the awareness that we *are* a soul - eternal, connected, and aligned with the Source, we begin to dissolve the mortal illusions and constructs that bind us.

We no longer chase meaning in external validation or transient pursuits. Instead, we turn inward, toward the quiet truth that has always been within us.

This shift is not merely a change in belief but a return to our natural state - homecoming.

In that sacred alignment, life becomes not a struggle for control, but an unfolding of grace. We then act not from ego or its many illusory mechanisms, but from love, compassion and clarity.

To live as a soul is to live in harmony with all things: to see the divine not only in ourselves, but in every face, every moment, every breath.

And so, the journey of becoming is, in truth, a journey of remembering who we are, where we come from, and what we are here to offer.

As we begin to recognise the soul's eternal nature, we also must confront the forces that distort our perception and block its true expression.

While the soul seeks harmony, the ego thrives on separation, fear, and illusion. It whispers lies that cloud our inner voice, leading us astray from a purposeful life.

In the next chapter, we will explore how the ego, in its myriad forms, strips us of the very potential that resides within - diverting us from the truth of who we are and trapping us in cycles of discontent.

At the same time, although the ego can cast a veiling presence over our true nature, it is important to recognise that by understanding our egotistical traits, we can foster greater self-awareness and self-mastery.

After all, this is a pilgrimage to reunite with the divine essence within and there may be many twists and turns before we arrive.

And yet, for the soul to fully express itself, it must contend with the greatest obstacle on its path: the ego - master of illusion and distortion.

Let us now meet our greatest enemy.

CHAPTER THREE
Beware the Enemy of Our Soul

A man likes to believe that he is the master of his soul. But as long as he is unable to control his moods and emotions, or to be conscious of the myriad secret ways in which unconscious factors insinuate themselves into his arrangements and decisions, he is certainly not his own master.

~ Carl Jung ~

When we are born, we do not arrive with an ego. We arrive with a pure soul and an infant body – nothing more.

As time passes, the ego creates and collects various belief systems, dreams, laws, thoughts and emotions.

And when we finish this life, as we all will, and return to the Source of all life, we will leave behind an aged body and all the ego's various mechanisms and machinations. The ego will die.

But what is the ego?

The Latin origin of ego, when translated, literally means "I."

However, this is not how ancient civilisations viewed the 'I'. These civilisations often had strong social and moral frameworks that emphasised the importance of virtue, honour, and social harmony.

These frameworks influenced how individuals understood their sense of self and their role in society, potentially shaping the way they experienced and expressed their ego.

As famously stated in Alexandre Dumas' novel The Three Musketeers, *"All for one and one for all."*

In many historical and cultural contexts, the concept of self was intrinsically linked to the tribe, clan, and community to which one belonged, effectively forming a collective ego.

This collective sense of identity often shaped the way individuals perceived their roles within society.

On a bigger scale, the collective ego can shape how societies and nations relate to each other - often bringing people together on the inside while creating a sense of competition or even tension with those on the outside.

The ego doesn't just influence how we see ourselves as individuals; it also plays a big part in who gets included or left out, and how different groups get along (or don't).

The collective ego finds its identity in sameness. Stepping outside this sameness makes one a black sheep – an outlier.

Consequently, nations, religious and spiritual groups, and various themed clubs and associations often base their values and belief systems on curbing or repressing the individual ego to maintain unity.

However, while collective identity often emphasises conformity, ancient philosophical ideas began to value individual reflection.

The ancient Greek inscription *'Know thyself'* at the Temple of Apollo at Delphi suggests a focus on introspection and self-understanding, which remains a key aspect of the ego's function in modern psychology.

This maxim encouraged individuals to examine their motivations, beliefs, and values, fostering a sense of self-awareness and agency.

Building on this introspective tradition, modern psychology, particularly through the work of Sigmund Freud, delved deeper into the human psyche.

Freud's theories shifted the focus from external social roles to the inner conflicts and drives that shape individual identity, fundamentally redefining the concept of the ego.

While Freud's insights laid the groundwork for understanding the ego's complexity, modern psychology has since expanded and refined these ideas.

Today, the ego is often seen as an individual's self-concept or identity, encompassing thoughts, beliefs, and perceptions about oneself.

It can manifest in various ways, ranging from a healthy sense of personal identity to, at times, an inflated sense of self-importance.

However, this raises an important question: How does the ego prevent us from listening to the soul's quiet, still voice - and why?

To understand this, we must first recognise that the constructs of the ego are, by their very nature, a shifting platform - capable of morphing, flexing, camouflaging, deceiving, and harnessing subjectivity to meet its needs.

This adaptability allows the ego to protect and reinforce the self-concept, often in response to perceived threats or challenges. The greater the perceived threat, the more robust the ego's response.

However, it is important to understand that the ego is not real. While we can create ego constructs, they lack real substance or worth. The ego diverts us from getting to know our soul – our true self.

In truth, we could say that the ego presents others with a distorted reflection of our authentic self. What they see is not who we truly are, but a carefully constructed image, crafted to preserve our sense of worth and significance in the world.

But if your self-esteem depends on anything external - status, approval, possessions, appearance - then you are building your house on shifting sand.

Sooner or later, it will crumble.

These external constructs can form at an early age, primarily as defence mechanisms against the various negative influences we encounter during childhood – at school, at home, with friends and in social settings.

As we grow older, we may build upon these early ego constructs, introducing new and more complex ones to help us navigate adult life.

The more we validate and cling to these constructs, the more likely they are to become accepted ways of living, distancing us further from a meaningful and conscious connection with our true spirit.

So, what are these external constructs? Below are some of the most common, each with its own subsets, variations, and hidden agendas.

At the root of these ego constructs lies fear.

Examples include vanity, projecting blame onto others, rationalising poor behaviour, repressing differing viewpoints, displacing responsibility, being two-faced, sublimation, imitation of others, intellectual snobbery, childishness, and resentment.

These constructs serve the ego by shielding it from uncomfortable truths, but they can also hinder personal growth and meaningful connection with others.

For example, imagine a man who consistently refuses to apologise to his family, despite knowing at some conscious level that his behaviour or attitude is fundamentally wrong.

Over time, his actions create resentment, emotional distance, and, at worst, contempt. This is a man who has internalised a patriarchal belief that apologising is a sign of weakness.

What he fears, at a fairly deep level, is a perceived loss of masculinity - an irony, considering that had he apologised, his masculinity and standing would likely have been evident to those receiving the apology.

Egocentricity and fear often go hand in hand, as both rely on subjectivity for their existence, making them natural bedfellows.

Unfortunately, many people foster a sense of realism around things that are not real, and this robs them of true happiness.

If you objectively consider your life, you may discover that aspects of your daily routines - your constant to-ing and fro-ing, can leave you feeling unhappy, discontented, or even purposeless.

These feelings are manifestations of the ego, which places pessimistic and negative barriers in your path; barriers that your soul knows do not exist.

You see, the soul cannot perceive, and the ego cannot know.

And yet, the opposite is also true: the soul is the embodiment of your worth, potential, and true identity. All of which are grounded in truth, in an indelible knowing. Hence, the soul always knows.

The ego, by contrast, can never know the truth, because its entire world is built on illusion and distorted perceptions.

You can catch the ego in a lie when you ask yourself three questions:

- What is it that you truly see?
- What is it that you truly feel?
- What is it that you truly think?
-

What is it that you truly see?

There are two key features of how we see the world that really matter: perception and perspective.

Perception is largely internal and instinctive. It refers to what you believe is happening or how something feels to you.

It shapes your experience of reality and is influenced by past experiences, emotions, and cognitive biases.

When you are faced with a highly charged situation, your perception is often unconsciously guided by a desire to feel safe—a response that may be amplified by past experiences.

Perception operates moment to moment, but it can be influenced and regulated by adopting an objective perspective. This kind of awareness allows you to stay grounded in the present - in the now.

Being in the now helps prevent perception from being distorted by past experiences or imagined futures. Living in the present offers a gateway to perspective - one that is free from judgement of self or others.

This state of awareness allows for personal growth, openness, compromise, sacrifice, and forgiveness.

In contrast, perception can sometimes be self-serving, judgemental, and damaging to self-confidence and self-esteem.

When shaped by fear, insecurity, or unresolved past experiences, perception may lead to distorted interpretations of events or other people's intentions.

This can foster defensiveness, mistrust, and a tendency to project one's own assumptions onto others. Left unchecked, these patterns can create emotional barriers, strain relationships, and limit our capacity to grow or adapt.

Such dynamics are especially pronounced in those who experience attachment anxiety - each attachment style casting its own distinct traumatic shadow.

Recognising when perception is clouded in this way is a crucial step towards cultivating greater self-awareness, emotional resilience and healing.

We can support this process by practising mindfulness, challenging the cognitive biases we hold, and developing key aspects of our emotional intelligence.

Together, these practices help guide and shape our perspectives, allowing us to engage with life more openly and authentically.

Perspective, on the other hand, is the point of view or mental framework through which you interpret something.

It is the lens through which you see the world, often involving more conscious thought and reflection.

Both perception and perspective influence how we understand ourselves and the world around us.

However, perspective tends to offer a more balanced and objective view compared to the often visceral and emotionally charged nature of perception.

Therefore, when reflecting on yourself, it's valuable to do so from a deeper, more balanced perspective.

This approach enables you to apply the appropriate type and depth of emotion, while also helping you to monitor and regulate your thoughts more effectively.

Developing perspective is a skill that can be nurtured over time. For example, engaging in reflective journaling helps you step back and observe your thoughts and experiences from a broader viewpoint.

You might also read more widely - especially across cultures, philosophies, and life stories or seek feedback from trusted others. This encourages openness to constructive challenge, which can reveal blind spots in your thinking.

Finally – and perhaps most importantly; practice empathy.

Consciously imagining life from another's point of view deepens your capacity to understand situations beyond your immediate emotional reactions.

This simple act of human and spiritual generosity can transform many aspects of your life, because its root is grounded in the soul – which, as I've previously described, is pure love.

At its core, empathy meets the underlying need for interpersonal harmony and meaningful connection.

What is it that you truly feel?
Within split seconds, what we see in our world is transmitted to the emotional brain - a legacy of humankind's existence in the hostile environment of prehistoric earth.

In modern times, this is both a blessing and a curse. Unlike our early ancestors, we are no longer faced with fierce creatures, hazardous environments, or food scarcity.

However, our emotions are now subject to the complex dynamics of the workplace, financial pressures, environmental change, social media, and the nuanced strains of modern relationships.

If we also add to the mix the modern phenomenon of seeking the perfect life - whatever that means - where personal appearance, possessions, security, and likeability are *de rigueur*, we find that our emotions can feel under constant bombardment.

But this bombardment is a choice.

Feelings that are invoked by negative perceptions are, by their very nature, features of the ego and by direct correlation, self-created.

If we feel inadequate, it is the ego's choice. If we believe we are not good enough, that too is the ego's choice. And if we are belittled, slighted, spitefully used, or betrayed by another, it is the ego that chooses to hold on to the emotional pain.

Of course, there are emotions that seem to slowly deconstruct our well-being and at times, even our sanity. These emotions feed hopelessness and draw us further away from our true heart-centre.

It is equally important to understand that while the ego cannot damage the soul, the emotions it generates can materially harm the body - particularly the heart. Hence expressions like heartbroken, heavy-hearted, heart-wrenching and downhearted.

These heart-sick states arise because the ego thrives when we accept fear, or the idea of loss, into our lives.

This creative mechanism of the ego is adept at whispering, "We have no control," or "We have no choice."

However, our spirit is indifferent to these ego-driven emotions and mechanisms, because it already knows that you are perfect, and that nothing can truly harm you.

Your soul is indifferent not out of coldness, but because it resides in a place of peace and wholeness. At your core, you are impervious to all that is material because you are an immaterial being.

You are eternal.

Although the soul feels none of these emotions, intense emotional states can cause a disconnection from it, as our feelings drown out the spirit's voice of comfort and reassurance.

This voice offers eternal reassurance: that nothing can truly harm us, and that by shutting out the ego, we can begin to heal.

We must remember that negative emotions will remain until they are acknowledged and then channelled into something healthier, more productive, and more harmonious.

This is achieved by moving closer to your loving centre and, by direct correlation, further away from the ego.

To move closer to that loving centre, we must begin by cultivating gentle self-awareness - learning to observe our inner world with compassion rather through the lens of harsh or subjective judgement.

In the quiet spaces between emotional surges, we begin to reconnect with the truth of who we are beneath the noise.

It is in these moments that we are offered a choice: to follow the well-worn path of fear shaped by the ego, or to look more deeply and tenderly at what we feel.

The emotions we experience may be intense, but they are not always what they seem. Often, they are shaped by past wounds, imagined losses, or stories the ego repeats to keep us small.

So, pause for a moment. Take a breath. And ask yourself, gently: What is this feeling – truly and is it shaped by fear, or by something deeper?

What is it that you truly think?
As human beings, we are immersed in a constant flow of thoughts - it is said we have between 60,000 and 70,000 each day.

Yet research tells us that most of these arise from the restless mind: worries, regrets, self-judgement, looping memories, and fleeting distractions. Very few are born of stillness or truth.

This calls us to ask: in the midst of all this noise, when do we pause long enough to listen... truly listen, to the quiet voice of the beautiful soul within?

Because if we truly listened to the thoughts and narrative of the soul, we would be amazed by the non-judgemental, loving, and inspiring song it offers.

The soul - our spirit - must use a mortal mechanism to get our attention. To do this, it employs the resources of the mind - our thoughts and emotions.

When negative and destructive thoughts and emotions infiltrate the mind, the soul's voice is drowned out — hijacked by the ego and its relentless need to be right and to be heard.

The often caustic and unnecessary negative chatter originating from the ego is simply a way of convincing us that we and others are somehow flawed.

We hold ourselves and others to account by employing thin-sliced, self-serving standards and beliefs, often grounded in subjectivity, fear and a myopic view of the facts.

This state is further compounded when we actively reinforce negative views - especially of ourselves - through comparison, the opinions of others, societal pressures, and past mistakes.

However, regardless of what we think, we must remember that the soul does not register or accept any constructs of the ego: it can only know the truth of who we are.

Our thoughts and emotions fluctuate between the objective and the subjective. These fundamental aspects of our humanity govern so many areas of our lives - most notably, whether we experience happiness and inner peace.

When we move closer to that loving centre called the soul, we begin to cultivate honest self-awareness; learning to observe our inner world without judgement or fear.

So, pause for a moment and ask yourself: What is it that you truly think? What is it that you truly feel?

Is your immediate world a tapestry of negative thoughts and self-judgements? If so, this is the work of the ego. If you feel you are not good enough in any aspect of your life, that too is the ego.

If you experience emotions that drag you down, or if you readily accept the negative emotions of others, that is also the ego at play.

When we follow the ego's lead, unhappiness and discord follow close behind. The ego is never satisfied - but you hold the power to stop feeding it and return to the stillness of your soul.

If we let go of the ego, we do not lose ourselves. In truth, the real self... the soul, endures long after the ego's illusions have faded.

Our soul exists in perfect balance. It does not depend on external constructs to affirm its inherent peace and self-knowing.

These earth-bound constructs are merely tools of the human experience, perceived as necessary but ultimately inessential.

In essence, the ego is a misguided self-creation - one that attempts to shape our self-image according to how we wish to be seen, rather than allowing us to simply be as we are.

It is a self-sabotaging mechanism, persistently undermining our growth by trapping us in rigid patterns of thought and behaviour. It binds us to illusions of superiority or inferiority, sameness or difference, lack or excess, better or worse.

The ego cannot choose truth, for it was not born of it. But you can - because your origin is not fear, but truth and love.

You are of the soul, and the soul always remembers what the ego forgets: that you are already whole, already free. You need illusions to live your life peacefully.

If left unchecked, the ego with its destructive autonomy builds defence mechanisms, rigid beliefs, judgemental perspectives, toxic comparisons, irrational fears, and escapist strategies.

The ego will do anything to protect itself and avoid facing the truth. And that truth is this: you are worthy, perfect, and beautiful.

We come to know ourselves only as we truly are for that is the only certainty we have. Everything else, including the ego's narratives, is open to question.

It is natural for the ego to resist once it senses it is being challenged. But it is not natural for us to obey its laws - ***unless we choose*** to believe them.

Daily Affirmation
I Am Soul

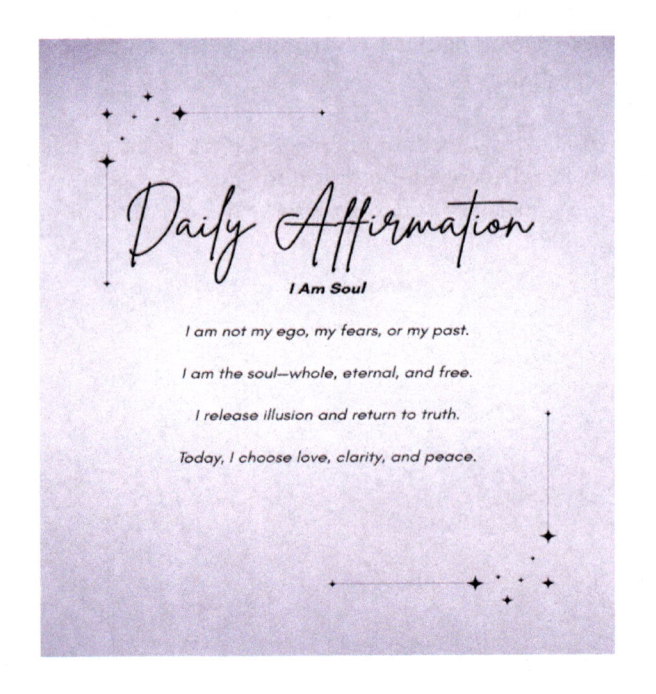

I am not my ego, my fears, or my past.

I am the soul—whole, eternal, and free.

I release illusion and return to truth.

Today, I choose love, clarity, and peace.

CHAPTER FOUR
What is it that the Soul really wants?

Intuition is the whisper of the soul.
~ *Jiddu Krishnamurti* ~

Humanity shares a deep, universal longing for one essential thing. It is the single ingredient that when present, brings purpose, happiness, connection, and peace.

When this ingredient is absent, however, the consequences can be profound. Its absence can lead to both chronic and acute emotional pain, as well as mental anguish.

That one thing is love.

Your task is not to seek love, but to uncover and dismantle all the barriers you have built against it and, by direct correlation, against yourself.

These barriers often take the form of fear, shame, unworthiness, resentment, pride, and the need for control. They arise from past wounds, limiting beliefs, and the ego's attempts to protect and separate.

In guarding the heart against pain, we
unknowingly guard it against love itself. To open
fully to love, we must gently release these defences
and return to the truth of who we are.

Truth lies in the awareness that you are love;
falsehood lies in all that the ego constructs to
obscure it. One is rooted in truth pure and eternal;
the other, in illusion.

And because you are pure and eternal, you hold a
unique insight and that is - the only true barrier to
love is fear – which is an illusion. And because
love is free of illusion it does not recognise fear.

It is a simple, though sometimes difficult truth to
embrace: our soul remains untouched by any
negativity we allow into our human heart and
mind.

Indeed, let us go further. Because we are love in
essence, anything positive, which is always born of
love - does not add to the soul, for the soul is
already whole.

When we accept or offer love to others, we are
simply being our soul-self. Complete, unchanging,
and beyond addition or subtraction.

In modern parlance, the idea of *"living your best life"* often suggests that certain aspects of the material world are aligning in a way that pleases us.

Yet one might suggest that these fleeting moments of happiness and contentment lack true soul meaning.

They are often based on external achievements, possessions, or validation - temporary conditions that rise and fall with circumstance.

In contrast, the soul neither seeks nor needs illusion; that is the work of the ego. The soul's singular desire is to see its embodiment and purpose fulfilled through the human form.

After all, the soul is an extension of the Source, to which we, as humans, are inextricably linked. Hence the spiritual truth: *'As above, so below.'*

Living our best life - and with it, lasting happiness - does not arise from what we accumulate or experience outwardly, but from how deeply we remember, inwardly, who we are: love itself, whole and unchanging.

Because the soul is unchanging and eternal it holds no judgements because this too is how the Source views its creations.

The soul offers no condemnation for errors or, as some aspects of the world call them, sins. If any error exists, it is simply the act of moving away from who we truly are and what we know at the deepest level.

This movement is not a rejection or denial of the soul, but a gentle drifting authored by the ego.

The feelings that arise from this drifting are not random - they are signals: a deep inner knowing that we have turned away from what truly nourishes us.

It is a kind of soulful homesickness, quietly unsettling our inner peace and disturbing our spiritual equilibrium.

So, if you find yourself experiencing emotions that are negative and fuelled by the ego, know that these are not signs of failure or imperfection, but reflections of having drifted from your soulful core.

And because the foundation of all healing is self-love, these feelings do not call for punishment or resistance. They ask only one thing of you: to return gently to the wisdom of your soul.

This call to return inward has echoed through the ages. Rumi, the mystical Sufi poet, once exclaimed, "*Oh, bird of my soul, fly away now, for I possess a hundred fortified towers.*"

This statement reflects a deep spiritual realisation: the ego's fortifications - *the hundred towers* – seem to imprison the soul. Rumi laments how these worldly structures, though seemingly protective, actually hinder true spiritual freedom and connection with the divine.

The hundred towers begin to fall when we listen to what the soul truly desires. And what our soul longs for is simply to be itself - unencumbered by the ego's defences, free to love and to be.

Being free of the ego allows the human mind to communicate with the soul - a soul that is in constant, uninterrupted communion with the Source.

When we remove the noise of the ego, our spirit, unencumbered, begins to whisper the truth of eternity. And that truth - the first truth - is love.

Love is the dominant frequency and energy of the Universe. All things are created and sustained by this truth, and we, as humans, are no exception.

The soul wants the human mind and heart to experience this first truth. From that singular experience, we no longer crave the ego's machinations - for we realise we are already complete.

It is this sense of completeness that has the power to dissolve the negative and the painful within the human experience.

Harmony and peace naturally follow the first truth; they are unwavering, indelible qualities of both the Source - and of you.

We must come to understand that everything we experience in life is seen and understood by the soul. But it is seen through an objective, all-learning lens.

There is no judgment. No matter the trauma and hurt, or the joy and contentment found in the human experience, the soul remains at ease. It understands from a perfect position of love - because it is part of the Source.

The human learning journey offers valuable knowledge to the ever-developing soul, but the soul does not attach the same meaning to these experiences as we do with human eyes.

This detachment is not indifference; it is deep understanding - an awareness that we are here on Earth for only a brief time. As the Bible so succinctly puts it: *"In the twinkling of an eye."*

What, then, does the soul truly want?

Not achievement. Not praise. Not safety. Not even happiness in the way the world defines it. The soul longs for one thing: the full remembrance and embodiment of love because in this way we will reconnect fully with the Source.

It wants the human self to return inward - to the quiet, sacred place beyond ego and illusion, where love is not something to be earned, proven, or sought, but something to be remembered as our original state.

The soul wants us to live not in fear of what we are not, but in the joy of what we have always been. It wants us to shed our false armours, not because we must, but because we no longer need them.

It wants us to know, with the certainty of light breaking through the clouds, that we are enough.

We have always been enough.

The soul's desire is simple: to express itself fully through your life - through kindness, presence, creativity, connection, and above all, love.

And when we allow this, when we say yes to the soul's quiet longing, we return to the Source in the most beautiful way possible - not only at the end of our lives, but here, now, in this very moment.

This is what the soul truly wants:

To be known.
To be lived.
To be love.

Daily Affirmation

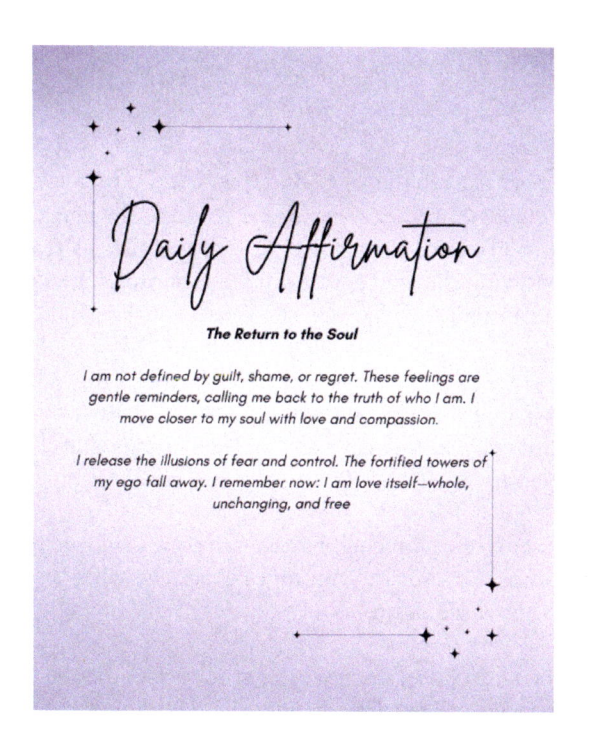

The Return to the Soul

I am not defined by guilt, shame, or regret. These feelings are gentle reminders, calling me back to the truth of who I am. I move closer to my soul with love and compassion.

I release the illusions of fear and control. The fortified towers of my ego fall away. I remember now: I am love itself—whole, unchanging, and free

CHAPTER FIVE
Let Go – Stop Holding On

You only lose what you cling to.
~ Buddha ~

There is a well-known Buddhist maxim that says, *'The root of suffering is attachment.'* One of the ego's most effective mechanisms for preventing us from following the soul's wise guidance is precisely this: attachment.

And what we are attached to depends on the outcome we want, or more precisely - what we think we want. It isn't just material things that we seem to attach to, it's the immaterial.

What we are attached to often depends on the outcome we desire - or, more precisely, what we think we desire.

The strength of an attachment (or attachments) often correlates directly with the depth and duration of the ego's influence.

So, it's no surprise that the deeper the attachment, the harder it becomes to detach from what is perceived as essential or important in one's life.

Material attachments might include:

- Wealth
- Possessions
- Appearance
- Status
- Comfort
- Physical security

It isn't just material things we cling to; we also attach ourselves to the immaterial. However, immaterial attachments are more subtle and often more deeply rooted.

These include:

- Beliefs and identities
- The need for approval or validation
- Control over outcomes
- Roles we play (e.g., parent, leader, victim)
- Past experiences or future expectations
- Emotional narratives like being right, devalued, worthy, or broken.

These invisible attachments are often the hardest to see, and to release because they shape how we give meaning to our life.

However, much of what we think gives us meaning - does not. The shifting sands of life externalise what does not matter because the very fact it is external should tell us that it is illusion.

The fleeting allure of a big salary, notoriety, good looks, a large house, or the pursuit of perfection - or indeed anything by which you or the world measure your worth, means nothing when war, redundancy, disease, or debilitating illness arrives. Chasing these attachments is like exhausting yourself in pursuit of a shimmering mirage.

These external illusions offer promises of a future, often with the belief that they are certain and unchanging. Yet the irony is this: we are not promised a future - not even another heartbeat or breath.

And as we know, the future cannot be controlled - yet many hold onto it as if it were guaranteed. To place our hope in a future veiled in mystery, shaped by countless unseen forces, with untold twists and turns is to lose sight of the sacredness and meaning held within the present moment.

So let us honour this moment with gratitude, allowing it to be filled with what truly nourishes the spirit - not what merely sustains the ego as it fumbles around for crumbs of meaning.

And what truly offers meaning lies within. It requires neither self-promotion nor over-compromise, nor the pursuit of others' approval. What nourishes the spirit is a gentle detachment from that which is illusory.

At the root of our resistance to letting go lies fear - fear of loss, of uncertainty, of a diminished sense of self. We imagine that our identity or worth will somehow be lessened, as though anything could be taken from, or added to, a soul that is already whole and perfect.

When we become attached, we forget that this is the ego at work - clinging, grasping, defining, holding on. Letting go becomes difficult precisely because it is the opposite of what the ego desires. The ego wants its fantasies to live, to grow, and never to die.

In this way, the ego will tolerate unhappiness and endure disharmony, simply because letting go is unthinkable. To live without this or that partner, without that salary or that house, to go without a cosmetic procedure, a romantic or financial safety net, or even a holiday - these thoughts become threats.

And so, we fiercely guard what we believe we need, even when it no longer serves us, and may even harm those we love.

It's as though we've been bitten by a snake, and instead of letting it go, we hold on to figure out why it bit us - only to be bitten again. And still, we refuse to let go.

Because the mind seeks harmony, we often fall into the belief that harmony must be absolute. We imagine it can only arise through total control of circumstances, people, and outcomes.

But attachment is born from this illusion, and total control, as we know, is not only impossible but also unnatural.

Perhaps we are being gently called to remember the wisdom of Wabi-sabi, the Japanese philosophy rooted in the sacred appreciation of what is imperfect, impermanent, and incomplete.

In traditional Japanese culture, Wabi-sabi is not merely an aesthetic - it is a way of seeing, a reverence for the quiet, the weathered, the humble.

It honours the cracks, the fading, the asymmetry - all that reveals the passage of time and the truth of our shared humanity.

It offers an understanding that material perfection does not exist. There is no perfect job, body shape, car, salary or cake recipe.

But Wabi-sabi is not confined to teacups, gardens, or worn wooden floors. It is a spiritual invitation, echoing through all of life.

A crack in a teacup, Autumn leaves scattered on a lawn, a blemish on the skin, a healed scar, a wrinkle, a curious habit, a missing limb - each speaks of life lived, of stories unfolding. They are not flaws, but features.

Not distractions, but doorways into a deeper kind of beauty - the kind that whispers rather than shouts.

And in this way, wabi-sabi mirrors the mortal condition: a fleeting, fragile dance where perfection is not found in what is seen, but in the unseen: the stillness within, the essence that remains untouched by time.

We do this by releasing the attachments that confine and consume us, welcoming stillness by settling the mind and living intentionally, rather than succumbing to habit.

For when habit leads, especially the habits of the ego - it is the tail wagging the dog.

So, take a moment and gently without judgement, ask yourself:

- What am I still holding on to?
- What do I believe I cannot live without?
- What, if taken away, do I fear would undo me?
- Are you playing a role - perhaps a version of yourself you're trying to protect?
- Is it a future you've imagined and convinced yourself you cannot live without?
- Is there a past you keep returning to?
- Are you embracing a belief, a relationship, an identity?
- What will you lose by apologising, admitting you don't know, excepting help or recognising there is much you cannot control?

Having answered these questions, perhaps you've begun to notice how the ego clings - not because it must, but because we often choose to follow its path. The ego fears disappearance, surrender, and the unknown.

The soul does not.

The soul will never disappear, has no need to surrender anything, and holds no fear of the unknown - for it is whole, and it knows all things, being forever connected to the Source.

So rather than forcing detachment, remember: you don't have to let go of everything all at once. Allow things to fall away - one small thread at a time.

Let us remember: by letting go you lose nothing. Letting go, is a sacred return to what is real, to what endures. To that which has always been waiting, quietly, within you.

Daily Affirmation

Letting Go and Returning to the Soul

I release my attachments both seen and unseen trusting that I am already whole. I no longer chase illusions of control or permanence, for I know they belong to the ego, not the soul.

What is mine will find me, and what falls away was never needed. I honour this moment, fleeting and sacred, as the only true home I have.

Like the crack in a teacup or the wrinkle on a beloved face, I see beauty in imperfection and peace in letting go. In surrender, I return to the stillness within—unshaken, unbroken, eternal.

CHAPTER SIX
Walking each other home

We are here to awaken from the illusion of our separateness."
~ *Thich Nhat Hanh* ~

It is said that the soul sings so that others may join in.

Yet in our modern, fast-paced world, it is a sadness that many have forgotten how to slow down and join in the song that celebrates all we share in common.

To cling to the idea that we are wholly unique and separate from one another is to overlook the many qualities that reveal our interconnection and our shared bond with the Source.

The ego perpetuates the fallacy of *me versus him/her and us versus them* as a way to create a false sense of meritocracy and self-righteousness.

This illusion of separateness breeds victimhood, extremism, dogmatism, entitlement, narrow-mindedness, and worst of all - a closed heart.

This is not to say there is no place for self-communion - those moments when we slow down, find a quiet space to be alone, and think, meditate, pray, or reflect.

Such activity is not rooted in isolationism; it is a reconnection with your soul and, of course, with the Source.

Our souls are on a voyage, and we are not sailing through life single-handedly. Along the way, we will call at many ports, visit distant lands, dock in unexpected places, and face squalls, becalming, unexpected storms, and tempests.

At times, we may even find ourselves in strange, uncharted waters. Yet wherever the winds of fate carry us, and whatever currents we encounter, we must never believe we are alone.

It is true, of course, that we can be with someone or even in a crowd and still feel utterly isolated and lonely. In such moments, we may turn inward, seeking to withdraw, escape, submit, fight, or even self-destruct.

Yet often, in these painful and disorienting times, we fail to recognise that our antagonist or antagonists - and the enmity they display is not a nemesis or destroyer of worlds, but a teacher.

The key to understanding this life principle is recognising that, often only in hindsight, we realise we've learned valuable lessons - about ourselves, the other person, their values, or the type of personality we encountered.

These lessons reveal what to look out for, what to avoid, and how not to repeat the same mistakes. In this way, whether by default or through a painful, even traumatic experience, they became a teacher.

They may not have taught us in a healthy, respectful, or balanced way but even the manner of their teaching becomes part of the mechanism that furthers our growth.

The challenge is to bypass the ego with this understanding. Without it, we risk becoming trapped in recurring episodes of victimhood, bitterness, unhappiness, self-judgement, and the desire for revenge.

We begin to reduce others to narrow-sliced judgments and reactive patterns shaped by the past - especially in future relationships. This approach is rooted in attachment.

By holding on to past hurts, we also hold on to their pain and the energy they carry. With one foot in the past and one in the present, we dwell in a place where healing trauma is delayed, and unlearning persists.

This is illustrated perfectly by the eminent psychiatrist Viktor Frankl, when he said, *"Therapy that is merely retrospective misses the point that the human spirit is oriented toward meaning and purpose in the here and now."*

And this is a man who knew the futility of dwelling in the past - having survived the death camps of World War Two.

Experience tells us that not every soul connection we make will be positive. And yet, we must understand that we are connected to every soul.

Again, Frankl highlights how we might respond to the afflictions imposed upon us by others when he said: *"Forces beyond your control can take away everything you possess except one thing - your freedom to choose how you will respond to the situation. You cannot control what happens to you in life, but you can always control what you feel and do about what happens to you."*

When we look at the great women and men of history, we see that many understood this truth at a profound level.

Take the life of Malala Yousafzai, who was shot in the head by the Taliban at age 15 for advocating girls' education in Pakistan.

Instead of responding with hatred, she forgave her attackers and used her voice to advocate globally for education, becoming the youngest-ever Nobel Peace Prize laureate.

Her grace, courage, and refusal to be silenced inspired even her former critics and enemies. She turned pain into purpose.

She famously said: "*I don't want revenge on the Taliban. I want education for sons and daughters of the Taliban.*"

Likewise, if we look at the life of Jesus, we see that those who feared his truth tried to extinguish it with hatred. Yet even as the world raised its hand against him, he did not raise his own.

He showed that love is not weakness, and forgiveness is not surrender. When he was wounded, he did not recoil in bitterness. When he was abandoned, he did not close his heart.

And when he was silenced, his silence became its own kind of teaching - one that still echoes: *"Forgive them, for they know not what they do."*

Perhaps herein lies the deeper meaning of those words because many people hurt others without fully understanding why.

Much of what we call harm does not always arise from malice, but from unconscious pain. Beneath the surface of a harsh word, a cold silence, or an act of betrayal, there is often a wounded soul acting out an old story - one shaped by fear, abandonment, or unresolved sorrow.

Trauma, especially when unacknowledged, settles into the depths of the psyche and weaves itself into the personality. From there, it speaks without words and moves without awareness, guiding behaviour like an unseen hand.

A person may act out of protection rather than conscious choice, from fear rather than love. They may not even recognise the harm they cause, for they are often asleep within their own suffering.

To recognise this is not to absolve all hurtful deeds, but to see through the eyes of the soul - to remember that every being is on a journey of awakening.

And while some walk gently, others stumble blindly through shadows they do not yet understand.

In that light, forgiveness becomes not surrender, but sacred clarity. Compassion becomes not weakness, but wisdom.

The mental and emotional walls we build often have their root in pain and to others, this pain this remains unseen.

In times of emotional pain, mental anguish, or deep uncertainty, the soul instinctively longs for connection - for a hand to hold, a voice to comfort, a heart to witness its struggle.

To reach out is human and it is a preeminent feature of our true soulful nature. Yet, paradoxically, this is when many withdraw and fall silent.

The ego, rooted in fear and illusion, whispers that we must go it alone. It fears vulnerability, for vulnerability is the gateway to truth and the ego cannot survive in truth's presence.

So, it crafts subtle stories: *"You'll be a burden." "No one will understand." "They'll think less of you." "You should be strong." "Why would anybody help me?"*

These quiet deceptions, among many others that can be cited, weave a veil of separation between us and those who would gladly walk beside us, if only they were given a chance.

Shame, guilt, stubbornness, arrogance and pride become armour we were never meant to carry. The belief that asking for help is weakness, or that self-sufficiency is a virtue above all, leads us not into freedom but into isolation.

And behind it all, the oldest fear: that our pain makes us unlovable, unwanted or to be pitied.

But true strength lies not in pretending we are invulnerable, but in recognising that we are never meant to walk this journey alone.

The soul knows this. It remembers that we are all threads in the same divine tapestry, each holding space for the other's healing.

To reach out is to return to truth. To say, "*I need help*" is not a spirit failed or broken - it is an affirmation of it.

It is the soul stepping forward where the ego once ruled, choosing connection over control, love over fear.

And so, in the quiet spaces between loneliness and the longing to connect - in the soft yearning to be seen, heard, and understood, the soul speaks an eternal truth: we are connected; we are never alone.

It whispers that we were never born to roam this life in solitude, nor to harden ourselves because of those who offer us the most difficult lessons about relationship, connection and life.

Our spirit remembers that healing comes not through resistance, but through remembrance of who we truly are beneath the stories, the scars, and the noise.

To walk this path with an open heart is not weakness; it is the greatest courage. It is a returning - again and again, to the sacred truth that we belong: to each other, to the Source, and to the vast, invisible web of the seen and unseen that binds all things in love.

And in that remembering, the song of the soul rises once more, not as a solitary voice, but as a chorus of awakened hearts, walking each other home.

Daily Affirmation

Today, I remember that I am never alone. I am a thread in the divine tapestry, connected to every soul and held by the Source.

I honour the quiet wisdom of my soul, which sings not in isolation, but to invite others into the harmony of our shared humanity.

I release the illusion of separation and open my heart to compassion, connection, and courage.

I choose love over fear, truth over ego, and healing over resistance. I walk this path not in solitude, but in sacred union with all who journey beside me.

CHAPTER SEVEN
Trailing clouds of glory

Listen with the ear of your heart.
Ignatius of Loyola

In his 1807 poem Ode: Intimations of Immortality, William Wordsworth pens one of the most celebrated lines in English literature about the soul's divine origin and its connection to the infinite:

'Our birth is but a sleep and a forgetting:
The Soul that rises with us, our life's Star,
Hath had elsewhere its setting,
And cometh from afar:
Not in entire forgetfulness,
And not in utter nakedness,
But trailing clouds of glory do we come
From God, who is our home.'

The human experience, as we call it, does not begin at birth or even at the moment of conception. The soul's journey to this incarnation begins in our true home: our eternal home.

In that celestial place, with spiritual clarity, foresight, and the guidance of many others - wiser and more ancient - we charted the path ahead.

For we have lived many lives, not only on this world but on others too.

There, in that higher realm, we chose various aspects of our impending life on Earth: our parents and family, our circumstances, our country of origin, and even our physical attributes and soul challenges.

We mapped out our life's path and purpose, along with the lessons and trials we would face, with the intention of staying true to our course and not being blown off track by ourselves or others.

Indeed, so passionate and committed about the lessons we should learn to support our eternal growth before coming to Earth, we willingly accepted the many challenges we would face.

With our eyes fully open, those who would become our greatest allies were known to us - as were those who would bring us our most profound challenges.

We were also aware of the law of free agency - the freedom to choose whether to stay close to our earthly purpose or to wander from it.

We would forget all the pre-earth discussions, trusting that faint echoes from the past would be heard in the whisperings of our heart - from our soul.

All of this, every decision, every detail - was made with love at its core and we accepted it all – willingly.

Why then, would your soul, knowing the many mental, emotional, and physical challenges it was to face as a human, embark on such a voyage?

To know this, we must begin by understanding and accepting the soul's true identity and origins.

Intellectually, we often speak of the soul's identity in singular terms - as a separate and unique entity, apart from others. A singular soul.

We may also consider and perhaps accept - that we, the soul, were created by something extraordinary: something Supreme and ineffable - a celestial parent, if you will.

Similarly, as humans, we tend to view life's chronology on Earth through a comparable lens. We are born to parents who conceive us, nurture us, love us, and eventually watch us leave the familial nest.

This perspective suggests a kind of separation: they are the parents, and we are the children - distinct roles, separate identities.

Yet both of these notional models drift far from the deeper, eternal truth - the sacred truth of Oneness. We were not created apart, nor cast from a distance by some far-off hand.

We were formed from the Divine Source itself - omnipresent, omniscient, and perfect.

Our origin, inscribed in the very fabric of our being - humanity's cosmic DNA - reveals what the soul has always known: we are part of the One, and the One is without end.

There is no separation. There can be no separation - for how can the wave be apart from the ocean? We are the Source, embodied for a time in human form.

And so, with this sacred knowing held deep in our hearts, we did not fear the journey from our eternal home.

We came willingly, and with clarity, because we remembered three unchanging truths:

- That we would never be alone - for the Source would dwell within us, always.
- That our time on Earth, when placed beside eternity, would pass like a breath, a single heartbeat in the life of the soul.
- That our return was inevitable, as surely as the soul remembers its way through the forgetting.

When we forget these three eternal truths, the challenges and lessons placed before us can feel far more difficult, as loss, fear, and vulnerability begin to take root in our lives.

Navigating these challenges often feels as though we must uncover hidden, hard-to-reach qualities - inner resources that bolster our resilience, expand our capacity to cope, and reaffirm our sense of self-worth.

And yet, the creative energy of the Source means we can move through the many illusions we feel detract from our soulful identity - those thought-forms and beliefs that cloud our truth and bind us to separation.

You are the god and creator within your own universe. You continually populate that world with forms brought into existence by your thoughts, and you animate them with life through the power of your will.

Each of us carries inner actors – archetypes, that can be awakened and shaped into roles. These roles often serve the ego by feeding on fear, loss and trauma. They are self-serving and bear no connection to the real you.

Among these illusory roles are the victim, the judge, the narcissist, the megalomaniac, the self-righteous rescuer, the boastful, and the uncaring.

To these, we might add the martyr, the chameleon, the perfectionist, and the shadow dweller.

It is important to remember that self-love and soul-centred living cannot take root while our energy is continually consumed by feeding illusions.

If we are never truly at home within ourselves - forever chasing the mirage of material attachments, the fleeting comfort of sensual pleasure, or absorbed in intellectual pursuits that reveal the outer world but leave the soul untouched, then we remain scattered and disconnected.

How, then, can we expect to gather the sacred energy within and return it to its rightful centre? How can we pour our essence out upon the periphery of life and still hope to carry its light within?

As the Buddha teaches, *"All that we are is the result of what we have thought. The mind is everything. What you think, you become."*

When we recognise this, we begin to see that illusion is not fixed. It is shaped by thought and can be unshaped by awareness.

In being aware and remembering the Source within, we reclaim the power to think, to perceive, and to live from the truth of who we really are - to create the life the heart desires for us. For that is where harmony and peace reside.

The heart is our creative centre. It is the heart that fashions the many textures of love. It is joy and sorrow, yearning and fulfilment. Hence: heartfelt, heartbroken, heart's desire, heavy-hearted, take heart, and follow your heart.

Love, too, is revealed in empathy, service, kindness, gratitude, sacrifice, laughter, compassion, friendship, and forgiveness.

True love is not a mere sentiment - it is a deeper knowing that the heart is where soul and Source commune. When we align with the heart, we align with truth, intuition, and the boundless creative energy that flows from our divine origin.

When we focus from the heart - centred on what we truly desire; the mind, the soul, and the universe align to make the impossible possible.

Fear, limiting beliefs, science, time, and space cannot contain the soul's creative heart. Through our divine design, we become the channel for what has yet to be brought into being.

Soul-centric thoughts and emotions do not need to be forced - for the heart already knows what it wants, without prompting from the human brain.

In this way, miracles gently reveal themselves, prayers find their response, and dreams unlike any other rise into view. Synchronicities - against all odds, begin to weave their silent patterns, and truths long hidden step into the light.

And as we know, no thought is needed to soothe a grieving soul or to show compassion to those in need, and no book can teach the sacred wisdom the heart already holds.

And when courage stirs, it is not the brain that leads but the heart, steady and unshaken, walking the path it knows is needed.

Too often, we allow the brain to overrule the messages of the heart - messages that may be exclaiming a warning, offering encouragement, soothing our pain, or gently pointing the way forward.

How many heartaches might have been avoided if the heart had been heard in the first place? So often, our *'little voice'* - that instinct, that whisper of intuition - speaks first.

But just as often, our noisy ego-brain talks us out of what we know must be done to cultivate a brighter and more harmonious present and future - to fashion the life we truly want.

Fear, hope, stubbornness, misplaced trust, self-doubt, and desperation, along with so many other ego-driven traits, hijack the one voice that truly matters.

The one voice that never misleads, lives in the present, never harms, and always seeks our highest good: the soul-centred heart.

Within that heart - your heart - lie all the resources of the universe, and all that we have gained through lifetimes of soul progression and experience.

And we are not sent to Earth without armour - nor, as I mentioned in the previous chapter, are we ever sent alone.

Spiritual armour holds greater power when we apply heart-centred effort.

Such armour includes unwavering self-belief, deep inner stillness, and the guiding light of discernment. Our shield is self-compassion. Our sword is truth. Our guide is love.

Courage cloaks us, humility grounds us, and gratitude keeps us close to the ideal and purpose of why we came to Earth.

These are not burdens to carry, but energies to embody - called forth not in conflict, but in alignment with the soul's highest purpose.

When worn with commitment, this armour does not weigh us down; it lifts us - reminding us of who we are, where we come from, and what we are capable of when our heart is fully invested.

As Rumi wrote, "*Your task is not to seek for love, but merely to seek and find all the barriers within yourself that you have built against it.*"

This is the invitation of the soul: not to strive endlessly outward, but to turn inward - to remember, to return, to reclaim this life's purpose.

Sometimes, turning inwards feels like an insurmountable task but in truth, in the quietness of our mind, where fear and doubt have no voice, it becomes a simple choice: a choice to love ourselves and no longer allow hurt, pain, or stagnation to disrupt our peace.

We must remember that we are not here to perfect ourselves, but to reveal what is already whole. We are not here to win battles, but to walk bravely through them, wearing the garments of love, courage, self-belief, and truth.

The soul is not in need of repair - it is in need of recognition.

And when we walk this path, clothed in the strength of our divine inheritance and guided by the quiet wisdom of the heart, we no longer ask, '*Will I make it?* - because we always knew the answer: *the journey was never about arriving, but awakening.*

Daily Affirmation

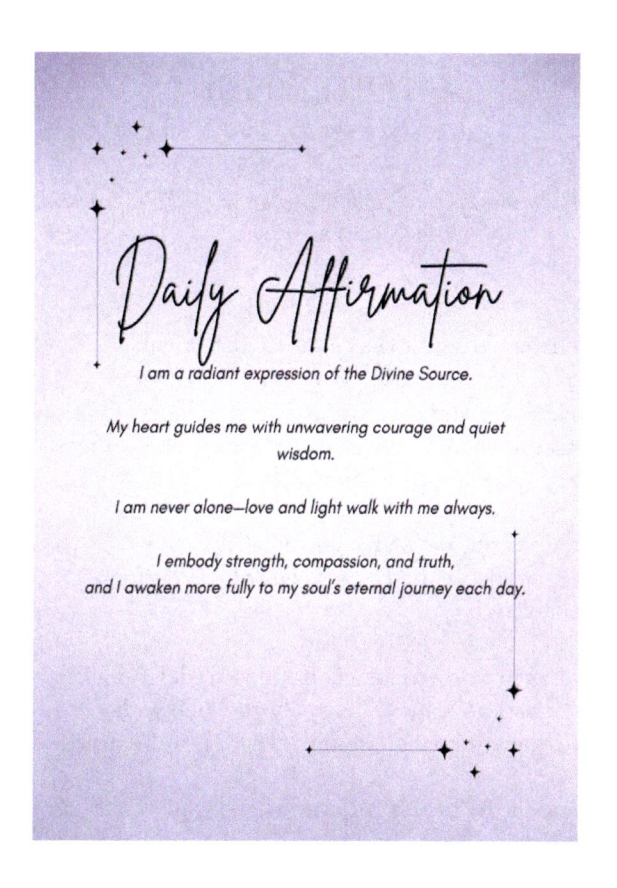

I am a radiant expression of the Divine Source.

My heart guides me with unwavering courage and quiet wisdom.

I am never alone—love and light walk with me always.

I embody strength, compassion, and truth, and I awaken more fully to my soul's eternal journey each day.

CHAPTER EIGHT
Listening to your soul's voice

When you do things from your soul, you feel a river moving in you, a joy.
~ *Rumi* ~

The ego's narratives can meander down subjective tributaries, delivering dogmatic utterances and cultivating distorted inner perceptions. Its voice can be compelling - often loud, persistent, and persuasive.

In contrast, the soul's voice has no such deviations. Its path is steady, true, and utterly reliable.

It has nothing to attack, nothing to defend. Our inner spirit is a love-born chorus, rich with wisdom and song - its only desire is to be heard.

One of the most profound challenges we face as human beings is learning to distinguish the ego's incessant chatter from the soul's quiet whisper.

One brings clarity and light; the other feeds on the self-doubting shadows we so often conjure.

Between the light and the dark lies a sacred resting place - a space of stillness where discernment is possible. In this space, we begin to know the difference.

One voice offers messages of beauty, connection, and truth, linking us to our celestial home, to others, and to our soul's purpose.

The other does not.

So how, then, do we decipher one from the other?

Firstly, we must recall that the voice of the soul is not one of earthly tones – it is of the heart.

Augustine, one of the early Christian theologians and philosophers is recording saying, *"Do not go outside yourself but enter into your own self; truth dwells in the inner man."*

Here, Augustine speaks of inner truth, implying that divine guidance or the soul's wisdom is found within - not through audible speech, but through inward reflection.

The first step in moving closer to the soul's voice is to recognise the distinction between it and that of the ego. This activity, in itself, can be a challenging exercise.

The ego's voice can sound reasonable, balanced and calming. Its ability to self-justify and soothe is a method of keeping you safe so that you can avoid difficult and sometimes life changing decisions.

And it is true that the status quo can often seem more appealing than the discomfort of shifting a belief system, abandoning a familiar sense of security, leaving a relationship, or confronting any of the many life situations that call us to be true to ourselves.

To discern the voice of the soul from the noise of the ego, we must first attune our inner hearing. There are three pathways that can guide us in this important task.

The four pathways are:

- Reason
- Reposition
- Reframe
- Reverence

Each approach serves as a pathway which, whether followed alone or together, leads you closer to your heart - and, by direct extension, to the quiet sanctuary of your soul.

Pathway 1 - Reason

Reason is our shepherd, guiding us to the safe enclosure of the soul - a place the ego cannot enter, where heightened emotion is softened and, if gently tended, can dissolve entirely.

One rational approach is to list the pros and cons.

At first glance, this method may seem simple—but it often reveals deeper truths. One rational approach is to list the pros and cons.

The cons, more often than not, are subtle machinations of the ego - designed to sidestep discomfort, elude courage, and settle for the illusion of safety over the path of soul-led growth.

Be wary, then, of the perceived disadvantages you highlight - they may soften the blow of a hard decision, justify inaction or avoidance.

While there may be elements of truth within them, and though they may seem powerfully convincing, press on regardless, for the truth lies beyond their shadow.

Here's an example that illustrates the pros and cons of a difficult decision: A woman, married for 17 years, lives in an established home with her husband and their two young children.

However, she is in a toxic relationship - her husband is repeatedly unfaithful. Both of her parents have passed away, and she has no siblings. She is isolated, unloved and facing a difficult choice: stay or leave.

Pros of Leaving
Freedom from toxicity
Relief from trust-related anxiety
Opportunity for emotional healing
Space to rebuild self-worth
Chance to model self-respect and boundaries for her children

Cons of Leaving
Financial insecurity
Difficulty finding a new home
Emotional impact on the children
Disruption to the children's schooling
Loss of mutual friends and social circle
Lack of family support
Potential loneliness
Single parenthood
Stress of divorce proceedings
Custody challenges

It's clear from the list that the disadvantages of leaving may seem, at best, deeply challenging - and at worst, utterly insurmountable.

In such a situation, who could blame the woman for staying - enduring yet more of the same trauma and toxicity?

And yet, here lies the rub: deep down, guided by the quiet voice of her soul, she knows she should leave. She knows she needs to go beyond the shadow.

In this example, as in many real-world situations, fear remains ever armed, ever ready, and stands as the ego's most powerful weapon. It limits choices and merely swaps one form of fear for another—disguised, perhaps, but fear, nonetheless.

Pathway 2 - Reposition

One helpful approach is to reposition the challenge you're facing onto a third party. Imagine a close friend in the same situation. What advice would you offer them? What support might you give?

You would likely recognise the inner resources they'd need to draw upon and how they might overcome self-doubt.

Such advice would come from a place of compassion, clarity, and a genuine desire to see them move forward in the best possible way.

And after all, this is precisely the stance your soul takes with you.

When practiced sincerely, this exercise becomes far more than a mental technique - it becomes a powerful inner tool. It allows you to step outside the fog of fear, anxiety, or indecision and access a higher, wiser part of yourself.

In imagining what you'd say to another, you bypass the ego's grip on your own story and tap into your soul's clear, steady voice. The one voice that holds only your true freedom and fulfilment in mind.

This externalised redirection creates space - space for clarity, for honesty, and for courage to arise.

Over time, this practice can become a habit: an important pause in the midst of challenge and turmoil. It is a way of grounding your decisions in compassion and truth rather than fear and doubt.

In doing so, you train yourself to become both guide and guardian - to stand in solidarity with your own soul, just as you would with someone you deeply love.

Pathway 3 - Reframe

You may also choose to sift through the ego and uncover the soul's guidance by adopting a higher, more neutral perspective.

For example, imagine watching your life unfold as though you were an observer viewing a character in a film.

What choices would you want that person to make, knowing you desire only the best for them? Would you wish for them to remain disempowered, fearful, diminished, or hidden?

Or would you want them to draw upon their inner strength - to face their fears with courage and resilience, and step into a fuller, freer, and more joyful life?

This shift in perspective, when applied with reason, loosens the grip of fear-driven thinking. It opens the way to clearer solutions, freeing you from emotional bias and unwise decision-making.

In such situations the maxim - *begin with end in mind*, is never truer.

If you can rationally consider a future fashioned by you making the right choices, then you will be surprised by how your spirit will galvanise the right inner resources and support you towards that future.

Pathway 4 - Reverence

Reverence is the root of stillness and the gateway to wisdom.
It forms a confluence of inner and outer awareness which, when aligned, offers unparalleled clarity—clarity through which the soul's voice can emerge, undistorted and true.

Inner awareness is born from reverence for silence. In silence, the soul finds its way through the mind's chatter and the illusory noise of the ego.
It is in peace that the soul resides, and in solitude that the heart finds rest.

By slowing everything down inwardly and seeking a quiet space - one undisturbed by life's busyness and its many demands - we begin to listen… truly listen.

PILGRIMAGE OF THE SOUL

No questions are necessary.

The soul, your soul - knows what you need. So too do the many guides, angels, and ancestors who commune with it regularly, all perfectly aligned with your personal growth and wellbeing at heart.

Within this inner awareness, inspiration and guidance arrive unheralded. The soul needs no fanfare - its message is flawless and unequivocal. Every word from the soul is pure and will never mislead you. Truth and love are its essence.

To arrive at this inner state in practical terms, some call the approach meditation; others, mantra.

It is equally known through the mediums of prayer, contemplation, and the creative expressions of writing, music, and art.

In solitude, it is found in the whisper of wind through trees, in the vastness of mountain vistas, in oceans both becalmed and stormy, in rolling green countryside, beside flowing streams and babbling brooks, and in the frigid silence of a desert night sky.

Nature is a spiritually grounding environment - something the ancients knew well and wove into the rhythm of their daily lives.

Inner awareness and knowing are also found in peaceful moments: in churches and temples, in a garden, a comfy chair, the kitchen, on a train journey, or even in the shower.

Our inner meanderings, once free from external distractions, may unfold anywhere. When we encounter this reverential quietude, we name it peace. Some call it reverie, others a self-hypnotic trance. Whatever name we give this daydreaming state, the soul calls it connection.

Whatever inner method or methods appeal to you, may I suggest you use it often. As spiritual beings in human form, we must remember that our spirit desires regular contact - so too, out human heart. To meet this need, we must carve out quality time for quietude.

It is in such moments that we discover peace, release, and healing. Wisdom beyond our years is unlocked, and insights stretch forth like glimmering beacons, illuminating our understanding.

The soul knows no bounds and is ever ready to share its gifts - all it asks is that you make time and choose the method that resonates with you.

As we turn to the matter of reverence in relation to outer awareness, we shift from the inner workings of the heart to the way we engage with the world around us.

While inner and outer awareness are intimately connected, it is our outer awareness that most visibly impacts others - often as a direct expression of our inner state.

When reverence informs our outer awareness, it reveals essential facets of our humanity.

These external expressions reflect how we perceive the world, interpret our experiences, and form beliefs about the people and environments we interact with.

They are not merely surface traits; they are echoes of the soul's identity or at times, shadows cast by the ego.

These external qualities include forgiveness, compassion, integrity, service, kindness, humility, patience, sacrifice, compromise, empathy, respect, honour, truth, and love.

Those who embody these traits seek peaceful living, cultivate gratitude, are slow to anger, and carry themselves lightly.

They are mindful stewards of the Earth and respectful of all life that shares our beautiful planet.

Such refined qualities are reflections of the soul. When we witness their absence, it signals a distancing from the soul, and by direct correlation, a distancing from the Source.

When we live in the present and are free from the influence of the ego, we draw closer to the soul by listening to what is most natural within us.

Our true nature is love and both the internal and external expressions of love bring us into a space beyond time.

This is why the past only carries the meaning we give it today and we are free to choose something other than regret or longing for the past.

The soul is an active participant in the present, for neither the past nor the future holds relevance. Time itself is of no consequence when you are eternal.

Clinging to the past dulls our inner listening. It yearns for what has already passed - the futility of should, would, and could, which only serve to tether us to what no longer serves our growth.

For example, there is no wisdom in holding onto grudges, in wishing things had been different, or in dwelling on what, at the time, felt like missed chances or betrayals of the heart.

It is as though, as humans, we often look only upstream, forgetting that the river continues to flow downstream - ever forward, ever onward.

Why linger in a world of memory that offers no tangible benefit to the here and now? Lost opportunities, failed romances, foolish mistakes, and fading youth are all part of life but they are not life itself.

Listening to our soul's voice is never a passive act, any more than the soul itself is passive. It calls upon our human self to resonate with that deeper presence, and this requires both energy and intention.

We must remember that every act of goodness we undertake draws us closer to the soul's voice. And we should never underestimate how even the smallest act of service can ripple outward - touching the life of the recipient and perhaps reaching others far beyond what we will ever know.

A great example of someone following their soul's whisperings is Marie Curie. She may not have spoken in spiritual terms, but her life was a profound expression of soulful service.

She listened not to the noise of societal expectation, but to the quiet pull of inner conviction; a voice that urged her toward discovery, compassion, and selflessness.

In choosing service over self-interest, refusing to patent her discoveries, risking her health to pioneer mobile X-rays in wartime, and empowering others to carry her work forward, she embodied a truth often spoken in spiritual traditions: that every act of love, however quiet, brings us closer to our divine essence.

Through tireless action rooted in quiet devotion, Marie Curie revealed that the path to truth and to service are not separate.

In serving others through science, she lived in resonance with her soul's deeper calling - a reminder to us all that every small, generous act is a return to who we truly are.

As she once said, "*You cannot hope to build a better world without improving the individuals. To that end, each of us must work for his own improvement and, at the same time, share a general responsibility for all humanity, our particular duty being to aid those to whom we think we can be most useful.*"

And so, the journey to discern the soul's voice begins not with grand gestures or spiritual eloquence, but with quiet sincerity through reasoned thought, compassionate reframing, soulful stillness, and reverence for both the inner and outer realms of life.

Whether through contemplation or action, solitude or service, what matters most is that we keep returning again and again to that sacred centre within. The soul does not rush. It waits. It whispers. It welcomes.

Like Marie Curie, and countless others who have listened not to the noise of the world but to the quiet pull of truth, we too are invited to become instruments of love and light in ordinary ways.

Each act of inner alignment, each outward gesture of goodness, brings us home to our deeper self and into harmony with the Source from which we came

The ego may try to distract, to delay, or to diminish. But the soul's voice is steady. It knows the way.

Daily Affirmation

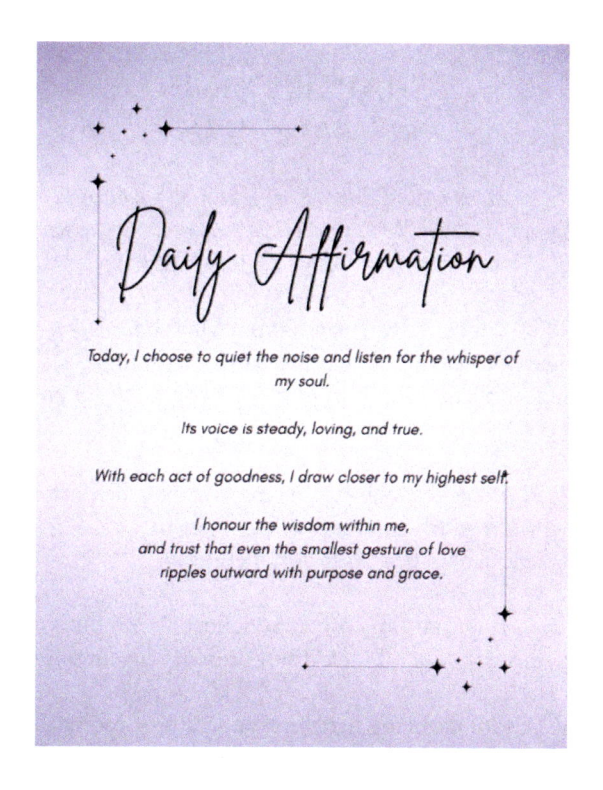

Today, I choose to quiet the noise and listen for the whisper of my soul.

Its voice is steady, loving, and true.

With each act of goodness, I draw closer to my highest self.

I honour the wisdom within me,
and trust that even the smallest gesture of love
ripples outward with purpose and grace.

CHAPTER NINE
Not blinded by the light

The soul does not die with the body. It simply returns to the Source, shedding the illusion of separation like a garment.
Paramahansa Yogananda

In 2008, a neurosurgeon named Dr. Eben Alexander contracted a rare form of bacterial meningitis that left him in a deep coma for seven days.

By all medical accounts, his neocortex - the part of the brain responsible for thought and consciousness had shut down entirely.

Yet during that time, he experienced something far more vivid and lucid than ordinary waking life.

He described being lifted into a realm of radiant light, held in the presence of infinite love, guided by a being he later recognised as his departed sister - someone he had never known in this life.

"You are deeply loved, he heard. You have nothing to fear."

His experience profoundly transformed his understanding of existence, leading him to conclude that consciousness is not created by the brain, it is something far greater, something eternal.

He also realised that the soul is separate and distinct from the body – that while the body's home is Mother earth, the soul's eternal home is with Source.

I wanted to conclude this book with a chapter that invites you, the reader, to explore how moving closer to the soul is not a rare or esoteric pursuit - it is a return to what you already are.

For some, this journey unfolds gently: through contemplation, prayer, love, or the slow shedding of ego.

But for others, it arrives unbidden, through an encounter with mortality that strips away all illusion and leaves only truth.

Near-death experiences, while unique to each individual, often carry strikingly similar messages: that we are not our bodies, that death is not an end, and that the soul is the essence of who we are.

People who have returned from such experiences frequently speak of a light that knows them completely and loves them unconditionally; of a peace so profound it renders earthly anxieties insignificant; and of a deeper purpose that calls them to live with greater compassion and courage.

Although such stories are described as metaphysical experiences, even that term can be misleading - for what is truly occurring transcends both body and language

A near-death experience is at its core not a physical experience, because of the physical trauma to the body. It is, in fact, the soul shedding its temporary housing.

Across centuries, cultures, and languages, this story among many others that can be recounted, reveal remarkably consistent themes - timeless truths echoed through different voices and vernaculars.

Each journey is nuanced - slightly different, yet deeply unique and profoundly meaningful to those who experience a near death encounter.

Their stories reminds us that the veil between this world and the next is thinner than we think, and that behind it, the soul waits patiently and without judgement to be remembered.

Whether through dramatic awakenings or the quiet unfolding of daily life, the journey back to soul is always available, always near, and always real.

Let me now share Mary's story - a personal account that echoes many of the themes we've explored, and one that, in its own way, reminds us how thin the veil truly is.

"I was recently divorced, and my friends decided that I needed a holiday to decompress from the stress and strains of the last 18 months. They arranged everything – we were to go skiing.

On the third day of the holiday, I decided to go off-piste. Although I had been warned by one of the guides the previous day that some off-piste areas were precarious, I was a good skier and decided to explore.

After about 30 minutes, I fell twenty feet into a hidden gully, struck some exposed rocks, and then tumbled another twenty feet with a lot of force.

When I came to rest, splayed over a rock outcrop, I immediately felt a searing pain in my right leg and chest.

I learnt later that I had broken my right femur, sustained a head injury, broken several ribs, and suffered a pneumothorax. The pain and laboured breathing were immense, and I soon lost consciousness.

Almost imperceptibly, the pain disappeared, and I found my spirit outside my body. I was looking down at my contorted form.

It was weird – I felt sorry for the body, but not for me. I was as light as a feather and free of pain.

I cannot recall ever feeling even close to this level of joy. I found myself in a dark tunnel. The tunnel felt somehow familiar, comfortable, and safe – and I had the feeling I'd been through this experience many times before.

I sped through the tunnel, although I didn't feel any gravity, G-force, or any kind of physical pressure. As I emerged from it, I was surrounded by the most beautiful colours – colours you never see on Earth.

And I know it sounds strange, but the colours
somehow exuded a certain tone that was in
perfect harmony with all the other colours and
tones.

Each colour seemed to carry its own energy –
frequency, if you will. I felt at peace – at home.
I felt like I was in this heavenly place, and I was so
joyous to be there. There were no concerns about
my body or what was happening back on Earth.

Indeed, my sole focus and wonderment was being
in this divine place where love was everywhere. I
cannot recall ever feeling even close to this level
of joy during my earthly life.

A tall Being appeared before me. He was
beautiful. He had big blue eyes – but a blue so
iridescent and changeable that I thought he had
stars in his eyes. His eyes exuded wisdom,
knowing, and compassion.

The light that surrounded him seemed like liquid
divine love. He was dressed in gold, and a deep
blue velvet sash was wrapped around his waist.

I felt like I had known him forever. He looked
ancient and young at the same time. He was awe-
inspiring, and I loved him without condition,
immediately.

The scene changed, and a large panoramic screen appeared. I saw a baby being born – I knew it was me. I felt the love and joy of my parents as I came into the world.

The scenes came quickly, as though time sped up, but not a second from my life was lost. Every emotion, thought, and interaction was felt by me – and I also felt the emotions of others with whom I had interacted.

All the while, this celestial being smiled at me with an abundant love – with not a single judgement or negative comment when I had not, as I perceived, been the person I needed to be.

There is no final judgement, and when you're in the divine light, you see who you are completely.

Underlying this review of my earthly life – from being born to the ski accident – was an awakening: an undeniable knowledge that I was eternal.

I knew eternal mysteries. I saw the depth and breadth of the Universe and knew that there exist dimensions, fellow eternal travellers, and spheres of existence we can hardly comprehend.

All, without exception, authored by the Source —
and love as the single binding principle weaving its
beautiful tapestry across the cosmos.

I chose to come to Earth to grow my soul through
loving myself and others. I know there is a divine
plan for Earth and all humanity — and most
wonderful of all, I am part of that plan.

And so, I knew: nothing will frustrate that plan.
But I can aid its fulfilment through finding and
living my purpose — by loving and learning as I go
through life.

The Being was joined by others, and I recognised
them immediately as my old teachers and guides
who had supported and prepared me before
coming to Earth.

They were my heavenly friends. I also saw my
grandparents, who looked youthful and vibrant.
Without a word spoken, I could feel their love and
respect for me. And I knew I was being given the
choice — to stay with them in my celestial home or
return to Earth.

The choice, as in all choices in life, was mine. But
whatever I decided, I knew I would always be with
them.

Although I yearned to stay, I knew I needed to return for my young daughter. I felt she needed my love. I knew she needed me to fulfil her purpose.

In the instant I decided to return, the light became even brighter and more loving – and almost immediately I returned to my body.

Mercifully, I was conscious only for a short time, but I could see I was surrounded by people in red ski-suits – the ski rescue team.

Various complications kept me in hospital for three months, and during that time I spoke to nobody of my experience. Intimations of that experience – and some I have not shared since – remain within me. Sacred and undisturbed.

Am I changed? No. I am what I've always been – eternal. But now, I linger closer to my soul, because that's my best part – that's my eternal part."

Mary's story, like countless others shared over the years, helps us understand that the phrase '*life after death*' is, in itself, misleading - because there is no true break in our existence.

We cannot deny, diminish, or dilute any part of the soul. We may visit many dimensions, live many lives - short, long, and varied but the underlying truth remains: we cannot die.

Near-death experiences offer a comforting insight into the way we return home after this earthly life.

Common themes include:

- The soul slipping away from the body, its role as an organic vehicle now complete
- A journey upwards and/or through a tunnel
- Arrival in a realm akin to heaven, accompanied by unconditional, omnipresent love
- Encounters with loving beings, family members, or departed friends
- Eternal knowledge and insights received, understood, and brought back to Earth
- A compassionate, non-judgemental life review
- A deep reluctance to leave this paradisical realm

- Upon returning to the body: a transformed outlook, newfound insights, the absence of fear regarding death, and a lightness in facing life's worries and challenges

These experiences are not hallucinations or the final flickers of a dying brain - they are glimpses beyond the veil, reminding us that we are not merely physical beings with occasional spiritual moments, but eternal souls having a temporary human experience.

The soul does not fear death because it recognises it as a return - not an end, but a homecoming.

What we call death is simply a threshold, gently passed, where love awaits, where truth is known not through study but through direct knowing, and where the soul remembers what the world made it forget: that it is held, it is known, and it is never alone.

Because death is not an end but a return, then it follows that the soul carries with it not just a destination, but a history - a thread of memory that stretches far beyond the current life.

While the body forgets, the soul remembers. One compelling way this remembrance has surfaced is through past life regression, a practice in which individuals, under deep relaxation or hypnosis, access vivid impressions, memories, and emotional imprints from other lifetimes.

These accounts do not speak of death as finality, but instead affirm the soul's enduring journey across time, offering yet another lens through which we glimpse its timeless nature and divine continuity.

After all, how can one lifetime be sufficient for the soul to learn all that is needed to fully realise its potential?

If near-death experiences show us where the soul returns to, past-life memories reveal where it has already been. Both remind us: we are not our beginnings or our endings. We are continuity.

In my role as a clinical hypnotherapist, I have undertaken many past-life regression sessions in concert with my clients.

What is remarkable about these sessions is how clients often come to see that their previous incarnations may continue to influence their present lives.

These influences and their historical roots can emerge from a wide range of circumstances.

I have worked with clients who suffered from a fear of water (*linked to a traumatic drowning in a past life*), attachment issues (*traced back to the sudden death of a loved one*), and lifelong night terrors (*connected to a past-life experience of being murdered at night by a jealous family member*).

Spiritually, these sessions affirm a deeper truth: that the soul does not forget. It gathers wisdom from every lifetime, carrying forward unresolved energies not as punishments, but as invitations to heal, to evolve, and to love more deeply.

The soul's journey is never linear. The soul spirals through time, gently returning us to the wounds that are ready to be healed, and to the truths we are finally prepared to remember.

The soul is dynamic, and its central desire is to be heard. And by being heard, wherever we are in our journey across lifetimes, we begin to meet the measure of our creation.

We are more beautiful, more creative, and more loving than we can fathom. Nothing is withheld from us, and the soul longs for us to know that.

Indeed, we are creators, and the world we design is of our own making.

Yet when the soul is listened to, it helps us fashion an inner and outer world filled with peace, purpose, learning, and love.

All we need do is embrace the idea that we have a soul and then listen to it and when we do, we do not become something new; we return to what we've always been.

Daily Affirmation

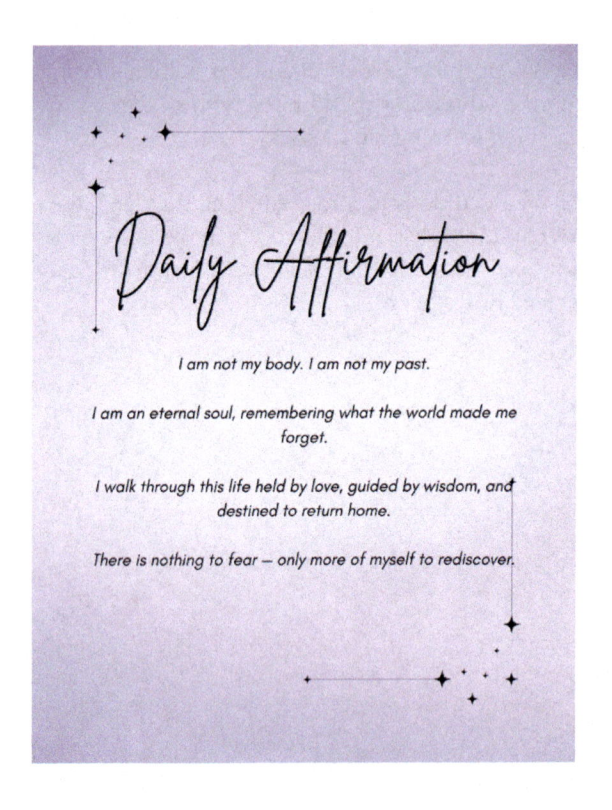

I am not my body. I am not my past.

I am an eternal soul, remembering what the world made me forget.

I walk through this life held by love, guided by wisdom, and destined to return home.

There is nothing to fear — only more of myself to rediscover.

CHAPTER TEN
Every Step Forward – Is a Step Inward

I searched for God and found only myself. I searched for myself and found only God.

Sufi Saying

As humans, we are respectful of the care we give to both our body and mind. We take care not to place ourselves in harm's way or to intentionally do anything that might damage our overall wellbeing.

We do this by avoiding risky situations, eating and drinking in moderation, choosing nourishing foods and beverages, guarding our thoughts against harmful and toxic narratives, and, wherever possible, finding ways to foster health in the body we've been given.

As the Greeks used to say: *mens sana in corpore sano* - a healthy mind in a healthy body.

However, as important as a healthy mind and body are, I believe it is equally important - indeed, even more so, to value the wisdom of the soul.

And the wisdom of the soul cannot be accessed without due care for the heart, body, and mind.

The soul speaks through the heart and when the heart is burdened by a body that is abused or demeaned, and a mind cluttered with unhealthy or toxic narratives, it struggles to hear that sacred voice.

This pilgrimage you are on invites you to walk a path guided by the soul, not by the vagaries and distractions of life, which so often conspire to steer you away from a peaceful, purposeful, and meaningful existence.

In my role as a teacher, guide, and therapist, I have found that there is not a single person who does not long to connect more meaningfully with their soul.

This desire is often self-arising, a quiet prompting of the soul speaking through the heart, stirring a sense of inner unrest.

That unrest translates into a desire for action — to do something that scratches the itch, to ease the yearning for *'something'* – often something different... but always something better.

But of course, to seek *something* suggests it has been lost. And yet, how can you lose what has been with you all along? You do not need to find something you have possessed your entire life.

This yearning often manifests as a desire to give back - to serve, to seek meaningful work, to love, to find peace - anything that soothes the quiet unrest stirring in the heart.

We look outward into the world, trying to tick the box that will make us feel more contented - more purposeful - when, in truth, what we really need to do is look inward.

These facets of unrest are stirrings of the soul. Yet the human mind resists being stuck, in a rut, or facing a lack of clarity.

Uncertainty unsettles the mind because it disrupts our perceived need for control and predictability.

But the soul knows better. It understands that time is irrelevant, and that if there is a pause - a space in the cycle of development or forward movement - this, too, is part of the journey.

And it is perfectly okay to linger.

The Universe is ordered and in perfect harmony. As part of that great work, we too - no matter where we find ourselves in life, are in step with the Universe.

This concept can be difficult to embrace, especially when we're in uncomfortable or painful circumstances. In such times, the longing for change can feel urgent because we want it to happen quickly, so we can move on.

And yet, people often find themselves in a holding space of their own making. More often than not, it is fear of the very change they long for that keeps them from stepping into a better space.

So, they wait for the right time. But stepping outside the familiar may not be as daunting as it seems, because the truth is, we already possess all the resources we need to move forward.

If you are sensing a need for change, it is your soul urging you to act. And why would your soul mislead, misdirect, or steer you toward danger?

In such moments, we must call upon the resources we've gathered along the way, whether through books, workshops, life experience, or the support of others.

Equally, there are parts of our personal makeup - dormant strengths and hidden talents that lie in wait, ready to help us move beyond the status quo.

This is why we so often hear expressions like: "*I didn't know I could do that…*" or "*I've never done that before…*" or "*Why didn't I try this sooner?*" and the ever-humbling: "*I have no idea where I found the courage.*"

You see, the soul knows your true worth - even if you don't fully recognise it yourself, and especially when others cannot, or try to diminish it.

It carries the memory of who you truly are - beyond titles, roles, wounds, and mistakes. While the world may measure you by achievement, appearance, or approval, the soul holds a deeper knowing: that you are inherently valuable, abundant, loved, and purposeful.

This inner knowing doesn't shout - it whispers. It is your alarm, your compass, your guiding light, and your most trusted voice.

It never leaves you. It is the root of all the goodness you possess. The soul wants your pilgrimage to succeed, and so it keeps you aligned with the path most needed.

And if, as we all do, you stray from that path, it will gently guide you back.

It does this through the intervention of others - seen and unseen - through moments of serendipity and synchronicity, and, on occasion, through a life-changing event.

2,500 years ago, Socrates spoke of a daimon - a quiet, inner voice assigned to him from childhood by the gods - that did not instruct him on what to do but gently turned him away from what was unwise or misaligned.

In many ways, this daimon mirrors the voice of the soul: subtle, unwavering, and often felt more in restraint than in command.

The soul does not coerce or clamour for attention; rather, it cautions, redirects, and gently nudges us toward alignment with our deeper truth.

Like Socrates' daimon, the soul's wisdom may arise as a quiet unease before a decision, a sudden clarity amid confusion, or a pause before a misstep.

Though easily drowned out by ego or noise, this inner voice remains our most faithful companion - ever guiding, ever remembering who we truly are.

And if we recall from the last chapter, those who experienced near-death encounters - especially the life review - often realise that it was the small acts of kindness and quiet gestures of love that brought them the greatest peace and deepest sense of fulfilment.

Here lies the great irony: such acts are not simply markers of our humanity, but manifestations of the soul's longing for us to connect with our highest ideals and truest worth.

We tend to believe that kindness, service, and sacrifice stem from our moral nature, yet they are - at their core - expressions of the soul.

In the end, this has never been a book about becoming something new. It is a book about remembering what you've always been.

A soul, eternal and unbreakable, quietly guiding, gently waiting. Beneath every question, behind every longing, the soul has been calling you.

Now that you have journeyed through these stories, reflections, and timeless truths, what remains is the most important step of all - to live soulfully.

To honour the wisdom within. To trust the quiet voice that knows your worth, your path, and your purpose. This is your pilgrimage: not away from life, but deeper into it.

Not toward something outside of you, but toward the sacred centre within.

You need not strive or search beyond yourself - the soul is already here. Your only task is to listen, to respond, and to walk gently, bravely, and in alignment with who you truly are.

You've wandered through stories and stillness, through memory and meaning. And perhaps now, the soul no longer feels like a distant idea, but a quiet presence beside you - familiar, near, and waiting.

So, what now? What do you do with this nearness?

You listen. You respond. Not with grand gestures, but with small, soulful steps - a moment of stillness in the morning, a choice made from love instead of fear, a kindness extended without expectation and the decision to forgive.

This is the language of the soul.

In choosing to live from this place, you honour
not just your own essence, but the sacred thread
that connects all living things.

The nearness becomes guidance. The whisper
becomes a way. And what once felt hidden begins
to shape how you walk through the world.

May I gently urge you to honour the earthly
pilgrimage you chose before coming to this life -
and remember: you cannot fail, and you cannot
fall short.

Finally, may I invite you to fully honour the
earthly pilgrimage you chose before coming to this
life - and remember: you cannot fail, and you
cannot fall short.

For each of us, this pilgrimage will one day end,
and we will return home. And in that return, we
will finally understand how hard the road has
been, how brief our time away from our celestial
home truly was, and - most importantly - we will
rest from our labours.

Until the next time.

OMNIA VINCIT AMOR

OTHER BOOKS BY STEVE

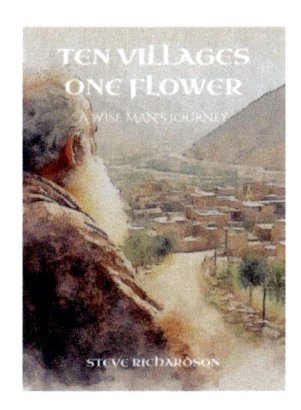

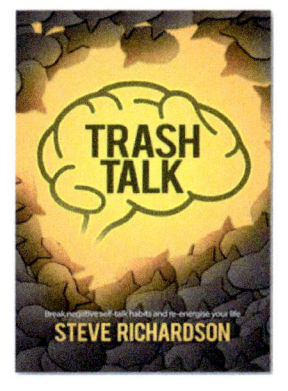

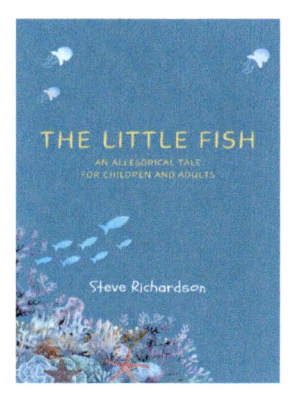

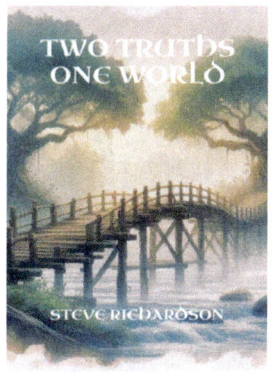

Printed in Dunstable, United Kingdom